PHOTOGRAPHER UNKNOWN
LOOKING UP HIS PEDIGREE, 1898

What can this terribly serious dog be studying so intently? A volume of Canine Jurisprudence?
Would it read, "Any object of food that falls from a fork, spoon, table, hand, or mouth shall
legally devolve unto The Dog." Or maybe it's a book on Dog Physics: "A door, when stared at by
A Dog, eventually opens and results in A Walk. Food always falls in a straight line, and the
angle described by the intersection of falling food and A Dog is termed a Right Dog Angle."

FUNNY
DOGS

EDITED BY

J. C. SUARÈS

TEXT BY

JANE MARTIN

A WELCOME BOOK
DISTRIBUTED BY STEWART, TABORI & CHANG

First Published 1995 by Welcome Enterprises, Inc.
575 Broadway, New York, NY 10012
Distributed by Stewart, Tabori & Chang, Inc.
575 Broadway, New York, NY 10012
Distributed in Canada by General Publishing Co., Ltd.
30 Lesmill Road, Don Mills, Ontario, Canada M3B 2T6
Distributed in the U.K. by Hi Marketing
38 Carver Road, London SE24 9LT, United Kingdom
Distributed in Australia and New Zealand by Peribo Pty Limited
58 Beaumont Road, Mount Kuring-gai NSW 2080, Australia
Copyright © 1995 J. C. Suarès
Text copyright © 1995 Jane R. Martin
Additional copyright information page 80

The publishers gratefully acknowledge the permission of the following
to reprint the copyrighted material in this book:

Elliott Erwitt's quotes from To the Dogs, by Elliott Erwitt, © 1992
by Elliott Erwitt, Magnum Photos.

Excerpt on p. 20 from Travels with Charley, by John Steinbeck,
© 1961, 1962 by the Curtis Publishing Company, © 1962 by John
Steinbeck, renewed © 1990 by Elaine Steinbeck, Thom Steinbeck, and
John Steinbeck IV. Used by permission of Viking Penguin, a division of
Penguin Books, USA, Inc.

Excerpt on p. 12 from "Snapshot of a Dog," Copyright © 1935, James
Thurber. Copyright © 1963 Helen Thurber and Rosemary A. Thurber.
From The Middle-Aged Man on the Flying Trapeze, published by
HarperCollins.

Excerpt on p. 28 from "Dog Training," in One Man's Meat, by E.B.
White. Copyright 1941 by E.B. White. Reprinted by permission of
HarperCollins Publishers, Inc.

Excerpt on p. 44 from "Verse for a Certain Dog," from The Portable
Dorothy Parker, by Dorothy Parker, introduction by Brendan Gill.
Copyright 1928, renewed © 1956 by Dorothy Parker. Used by
permission of Viking Penguin, a division of Penguin Books, USA, Inc.

Excerpt on p. 56 from "Confusing a Puppy" in Every Dog Should
Own a Man, copyright © 1952 by Corey Ford. Used by permission of
the Trustees of Dartmouth College.

Excerpt on p. 68 from "The Dog That Bit People," Copyright © 1933,
1961, James Thurber. From My Life and Hard Times, published by
HarperCollins.

Library of Congress Card Catalog Number: 95-060046
ISBN 1-55670-410-0

Printed and bound in Italy by Arnoldo Mondadori Editore
10 9 8 7 6 5 4 3 2

TITLE PAGE: JACK TINNEY
DOG COOLING HIMSELF, 1960

To celebrate the dog days of a late summer, this shot
appeared in Life magazine's August 25, 1960 issue.

W. B. Davidson
We Are Seven, Narragansett Pier,
Rhode Island, 1890

What do you say to a proud mother who also happens to be a pit bull? "Oh, how vicious your puppies look!" Or, "Just six weeks old, and already the terrors of the neighborhood. How cute!" Or perhaps just mutter "Nice doggies," while slowly backing away....

H IS NAME WAS CLIDE AND HE WAS THE LARGEST YELLOW LABRADOR YOU'VE EVER SEEN, PERHAPS TWICE AS LARGE AS THE ONE ON RECORD. HE LIVED WITH THE THAYER FAMILY IN A BIG HOUSE ON LILAC LANE IN PRINCETON, NEW JERSEY, AND WAS AS WELL KNOWN AROUND TOWN AS ALBERT EINSTEIN HAD BEEN TWENTY YEARS EARLIER. THERE WASN'T A BACKYARD HE HADN'T CROSSED, OR A POOL HE HADN'T JUMPED IN, OR A STATUE HE HADN'T BARKED AT. ❧ BIG CLIDE WAGGED HIS TAIL ALL THE TIME, EVEN WHEN HE WAS ASLEEP ON THE WOODEN FLOORS OF THE OLD HOUSE. THE SOUND WAS AKIN TO SOMEONE TEARING THE WALLS DOWN WITH A HUNDRED-POUND SLEDGEHAMMER. HIS SNORING WAS EVEN LOUDER—LOUDER THAN THE OLD GRANDFATHER CLOCK ON THE SECOND FLOOR LANDING, LOUDER THAN THE PRINCETON JUNCTION LOCOMOTIVE. ❧ ALTHOUGH CLIDE GOT ALONG WITH MOST OF THE DOGS IN THE NEIGHBORHOOD, THERE WAS ONE WHOSE VERY PRESENCE MADE HIS BLOOD BOIL: MRS. BURNS'S LITTLE WIREHAIRED MONGREL. WHENEVER MRS. BURNS CAME OVER TO VISIT THE THAYERS, LEAVING HER DOG TO RELAX IN THE STATION WAGON, CLIDE WOULD BE TIED TO A TREE IN THE YARD. BUT, MORE OFTEN THAN NOT, HE WOULD CHEW THROUGH THE LEASH AND ATTACK THE CAR, COVERING IT

WITH MUD FROM TOP TO BOTTOM. THE TERRIFIED LITTLE DOG WOULD GO TO THE

BATHROOM ON THE BACK SEAT. ❧ CLIDE'S TRUE NEMESIS—THE BLACK CLOUD OVER HIS

LIFE—WAS NONE OTHER THAN THE PRINCETON TIGER, THE FAMOUS BRONZE STATUE THAT

FACES NASSAU HALL ON NASSAU STREET. AT THE MERE SIGHT OF THE STATUE HE WOULD

FLY INTO AN UNCONTROLLABLE RAGE AND BARK HIMSELF INTO EXHAUSTION, CAUSING ALARM

THROUGHOUT THE WHOLE TOWN. HE HATED THAT TIGER TO HIS DYING DAY. HAD IT BEEN

A REAL ONE, HE WOULD HAVE TRIED TO CHASE IT UP A TREE. ❧ AS THE YEARS WENT BY,

CLIDE'S FORAYS THROUGH THE NEIGHBORHOOD GOT LONGER AND LONGER. HE DISCOVERED

A MUDHOLE SOMEWHERE AND WOULD COME BACK ALL MOIST AND COVERED WITH SLOP, A

BIG SMILE ON HIS BASKETBALL-SIZED FACE. MR. THAYER INSTALLED COW SLATS AT THE END

OF THE DRIVEWAY TO KEEP CLIDE FROM THE HAUNT, BUT CLIDE, OF COURSE, LEARNED TO

LEAP OVER THEM. ❧ AROUND THE HOLIDAYS, CLIDE WORE A SANTA CLAUS HAT. HE

LOOKED SO FUNNY THAT A COUPLE OF DRIVERS WERE KNOWN TO HAVE ACTUALLY DRIVEN

ONTO THE SIDEWALK WHEN THEY SAW HIM CROSS THE STREET. SOME WOULD EVEN SWEAR

THAT THE DOG TURNED AROUND AND SMILED AT THEM.—_J.C. SUARÈS_

Watson: Is there any point to which you would wish to draw my attention?

Holmes: To the curious incident of the dog in the night-time.

Watson: The dog did nothing in the night-time.

Holmes: That was the curious incident.

....

SIR ARTHUR CONAN DOYLE
The Memoirs of Sherlock Holmes

BRUCE DAVIDSON
ENGLAND, 1960

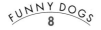

RICHARD KALVAR
NEW YORK, 1976

The first time he ever saw a body of water, he trotted nervously along the steep bank for a while, fell to barking wildly, and finally plunged in from a height of eight feet or more. I shall always remember that shining, virgin dive. Then he swam upstream and back just for the pleasure of it, like a man. It was fun to see him battle upstream against a stiff current, growling every foot of the way. He had as much fun in the water as any person I have ever known. You didn't have to throw a stick into the water to get him to go in. Of course, he would bring back a stick if you did throw one in. He would have brought back a piano if you had thrown one in.

....

JAMES THURBER
Snapshot of a Dog

KARL BADEN
MAN AND DOG, REVERE BEACH,
MASSACHUSETTS, 1981

I was out on the beach on the North Shore of Massachusetts. There was a fellow and his dog watching the planes come in low. They seemed very absorbed.

Dog, n. *A kind of additional or subsidiary Deity designed to catch the overflow and surplus of the world's worship. This Divine Being in some of his smaller and silkier incarnations takes, in the affection of Woman, the place to which there is no human male aspirant.*

The Dog is a survival—an anachronism. He toils not, neither does he spin, yet Solomon in all his glory never lay upon a door-mat all day long, sun-soaked and fly-fed and fat, while his master worked for the means wherewith to purchase an idle wag of the Solomonic tail, seasoned with a look of tolerant recognition.

AMBROSE BIERCE
The Devil's Dictionary

LARS PETER ROOS
MIOJE, STOCKHOLM, 1993

One day I accompanied my neighbor, an old lady who has a Pug, on one of their daily walks.
I went because I really like that dog. A lot of old ladies in Sweden have Pugs.

BARRY MUNGER
LEAPING POODLE, WESTMINSTER DOG SHOW, 1994

They have cages off to the side, holding pens for the dogs. This dog just has a great vertical leap. It was very, very excited. Some Poodles just get excited and jump. Like a Cuban volleyball team—not very tall but they jump very high.

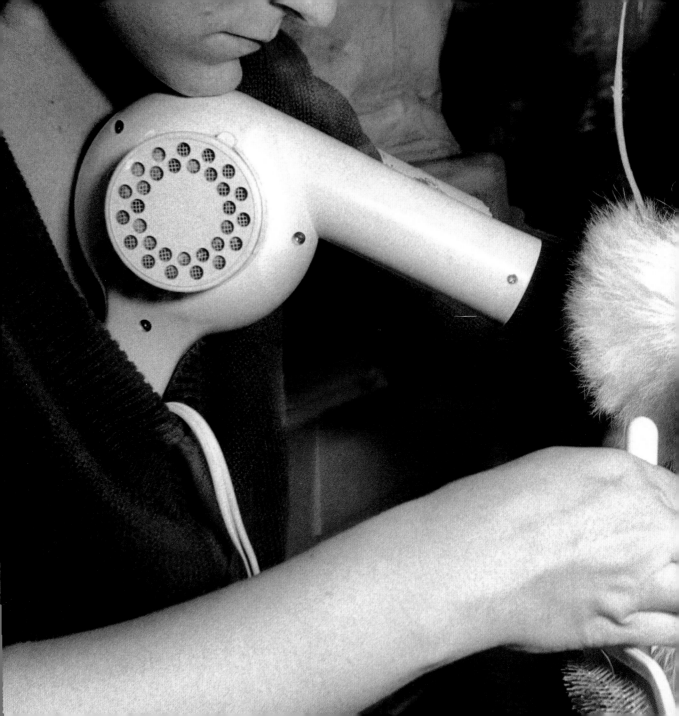

KARL BADEN
DOG SHOW, BOSTON, 1993

This was backstage, as the dog, who is not a Poodle,
was being prepped for the ring. He stood very still.
He seemed to be an old hand at this routine.

Charley is a born diplomat. He prefers negotiation to fighting,

and properly so, since he is very bad at fighting. Only once in his ten

years has he been in trouble—when he met a dog who refused to

negotiate. Charley lost a piece of his right ear that time.

But he is a good watchdog—has a roar like a lion, designed to

conceal from night-wandering strangers that fact that he couldn't

bite his way out of a cornet du papier. . . .

....

JOHN STEINBECK
Travels with Charley

CHAIM KANNER
HONFLEUR, FRANCE, 1968

Now this is an interesting story. I was near Paris, taking lots of pictures. I saw the Boxer
in the window and naturally pointed my camera up. But at the same time, Elliott Erwitt was
there, pointing his camera at me. So if this were his picture, taken from down the street,
what you'd see would be me, photographing this dog.

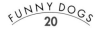

LAURA BAKER-STANTON
ACIE'S JUST MADE IT, 1993

*They call her Mada. She's the sweetest doll of a dog. She was
at a dog show in Tulsa, competing with all the other Bull
Terriers. I don't know if she won anything or not.*

WALTER CHANDOHA
WESTMINSTER DOG SHOW, 1965

*The Mastiff was just sitting there with that spike collar
and a look that said, "Watch out." But you know, looks don't
mean a thing, especially in New York.*

JOYCE RAVID
COSMO TIGER, 1994

This is his most recent official portrait, taken in the country near New York.
I don't know what kind of dog he is, but he's a nice dog.

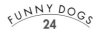

MARY BLOOM
NEW YORK CITY STREET, 1992

In Chelsea, I ran into a woman who had three
English Bulldogs, and the one I wanted to shoot was
the one who would have nothing to do with me.
But the woman was thrilled and proud.

It is not so much that I acquire dogs as it is that dogs acquire me.

Maybe they even shop for me, I don't know.

If they do, I assume they have many problems, because they certainly

arrive with plenty, which they turn over to me.

E.B. WHITE
The Care and Training of a Dog

CHAIM KANNER
MUGGY DAY, 1976

This was shot on Third Avenue and around 20th Street in Manhattan, during the years
when I used to spend the summer months in New York. The dog was not a lonely dog.
Its owner was in the supermarket and it was just waiting outside.
To me it looked very well taken care of. I think it was, mostly, a very hot dog.

ROBIN SCHWARTZ
MARTIN AND GUINEVERE, HALLOWEEN, 1987

They're Airedales, in their owner's costumes. I was very interested in Guinevere since she was very pretty. She was the younger one. But since they were a couple, I included Martin too.

WALTER CHANDOHA
BATHTIME, 1965

I was working for a vitamin company and they wanted to promote their new coat lustre product.
The shot called for a hairless dog, but it would've been so ugly. The Weimaraner was a good dog,
a well-trained dog, and he had a fine time in my bathtub in Annandale, New Jersey,
once he got used to standing on the porcelain.

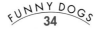

SUSAN COPEN OKEN
DOG WITH ATTITUDE, 1985

*She's just so feminine, the way she's striking the pose.
There was a performance piece going on in Central Park and the Chihuahua was just
sitting there, waiting for her owner to be finished.*

HANS OLA ERICSON
MONTPARNASSE, 1987

*This was at a café. I lived for many years in Paris, and this was a common scene.
The Parisians love dogs and cats. I like them too. It's wonderful to be in a restaurant
and watch the animals.*

HEEL!

This page: Maud Frizon metallic leather pump with a high, thick heel, about $295. The dog, a Shih Tzu; Prada leash, about $190. Opposite: Guess metallic leather shoe-boot, cowboy style, about $165. The dog, a Weimaraner. More info, last pages.

ELLIOTT ERWITT
NEW YORK CITY, 1989

These professional dogs have several advantages.
For one, they come cheaper than humans.

ELLIOTT ERWITT
BIRMINGHAM, ENGLAND, 1991

*You will often see a kind of relationship between English owners
and their pets that is so close it is simply unbelievable.*

JOHN DRYSDALE
NUTS ABOUT SQUIRRELS, 1975

Someone brought three tiny Grey Squirrels to Graham Hughes's farm near Southam, England.
They'd been abandoned by their wild mother and had to be fed every two hours with a syringe.
It was a laborious task. When Graham's Bulldog Suzie—whose maternal instincts had already
saved other abandoned animals—produced a litter of puppies, Graham gave Suzie the squirrels.
The only problem is that the squirrels have such a fearsome looking mother,
they've lost all their wariness. In a sense, Suzie domesticated them.

A skeptic world you face with steady gaze;

High in young pride you hold your noble head;

Gayly you meet the rush of roaring days.

(Must you eat that puppy biscuit on the bed?)

Lancelike your courage, gleaming swift and strong,

Yours the white rapture of a winged soul,

Yours is a spirit like a May-day song.

(God help you, if you break the goldfish bowl!)

DOROTHY PARKER
Verse for a Certain Dog

LAURA BAKER-STANTON
DASH, 1993

He's about eight or nine years old in this picture, and it's the only one
I'll ever get of him where he's not three feet in the air—let alone standing still.
He's a multistate frisbee champion, and doesn't laze around very much.

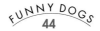

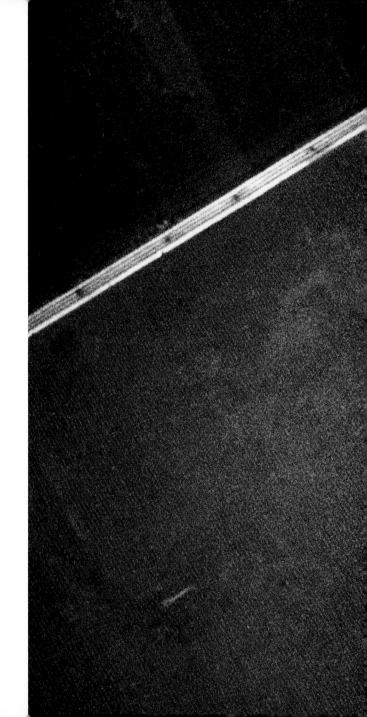

ANTONIN MALY
UNTITLED, 1989

ROLF ADLERCREUTZ
RECOGNITION, C. 1990

OVERLEAF: JACK JACOBS
SAMMIE, 1988

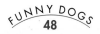

JOYCE RAVID
DOG SELLING NEWSPAPERS, NEW YORK, 1980

I don't know anything about him. He was just there.

PHOTOGRAPHER UNKNOWN
THE LITTLE RASCALS, C. 1930

One of the many pit-bull mixes who played Pete the Pup (and who would have had a fresh ring painted around his eye for each shoot) shares a festive moment with a duck.

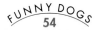

When a doting person gets down on all fours and plays with

his dog's rubber mouse, it only confuses the puppy and gives him a sense

of insecurity. He gets the impression that the world is unstable,

and wonders whether he is supposed to walk on his hind legs

and learn to smoke cigars.

COREY FORD

JOHN DRYSDALE
HAIRDRESSER'S HOT DOG, 1969

George Constantine's problem with his London salon
is that he can't get it into full production. His dog Rex, a
six-year-old Labrador-Mastiff cross, has taken up a seat
nearly his whole life. Most of the regular clients are so used
to it, they just ignore him. The curler and hairnet wig are
for the benefit of the new customers, who often ask why Rex
is under the dryer. Rex just sits there with a "humans are so
silly" expression and never bats an eyelid.

OVERLEAF: JOHN DRYSDALE
HOLLOW LAUGHTER, 1975

The strange animal inhabiting this tree trunk near Daventry,
England, happened while Trace Clunes was playing follow
the leader with Winnie, her Bulldog. Her grandfather had
just brought the log over for firewood and Winnie, who goes
into everything from a box to a hole, couldn't resist.

Things that upset a terrier may pass virtually unnoticed by a Great Dane.

....

SMILEY BLANTON

ALEN MACWEENEY
BACHELOR ON HOLIDAY, FIRE ISLAND,
NEW YORK, 1993

*He's a Jack Russell Terrier from Ireland, and very Napoleonic in character. His breed was invented
by the Reverend Jack Russell, who wanted a dog small enough to sit in the saddle, quick enough to
jump off and scramble down a foxhole, and strong enough to jump back up when the job was done.
Bachelor thinks he's a large dog. Walking with a five-foot-long stick that weighs about fifteen
pounds is an average task for him. He'd found the stick on the beach, maneuvered it up the stairs
by dropping it in the middle and taking its end, and was now in the process of taking it home.
We call him the King since he has such a grand attitude as he struts along through life.*

ELLIOTT ERWITT
NEW YORK CITY, 1946

*People like to point out that the photograph is taken
from the dog's point of view, but the dog, of course,
isn't surprised by that, as you can see. He's completely
ignoring the person next to him, and her point of view.*

ARCHIE LIEBERMAN
JUNIOR AND THE BIRD, 1988

*This is a true story. I came out the door onto the patio and Junior, my Golden Retriever,
was standing nose to beak with a bird. So I called out, "Junior! Stay! Don't move!" and rushed
into the house to get a camera. When I came back, my pal was still there, and so was the bird.
Which was not such a good thing for the bird, as the next moment a cat rushed up, caught the
bird and ran off. Junior ran after her, caught her and shook her until he released his
new friend. But the bird, who had wised up, flew away.*

JOHN DRYSDALE
LLAMA LOVE, 1969

*The llama, a four-week-old orphan at Longleaf Safari Park near Warminster, England,
had formed a remarkably close relationship with this English Pointer. The dog was a veteran of
surrogate parenting, having proved his mettle with lion and tiger cubs already.
He seemed happy to lend an ear.*

Muggs was afraid of only one thing, an electrical storm. Thunder and lightning frightened him out of his senses (I think he thought a storm had broken the day the mantelpiece fell). He would rush into the house and hide under a bed or in the clothes closet. So we fixed up a thunder machine out of a long narrow piece of sheet iron with a wooden handle at the end. Mother would shake this vigorously when she wanted to get Muggs into the house. It made an excellent imitation of thunder, but I suppose it was the most roundabout system for running a household that was ever devised. It took a lot out of Mother.

....

JAMES THURBER
The Dog That Bit People

ANTONIN MALÝ
EDA, PRAGUE, 1980

Eda belonged to some married friends of mine, Michaela and Peter. She was a present from Peter for Michaela, who was about to have a child in the hospital. It took two strong men to get the dog onto the bookshelf. Their fee was eight pork sausages—a Czech national food.

The famous director of such thrillers as Spellbound *and* The 39 Steps *was known to be
fond of terriers such as this Sealyham. His indomitable companions were treated with great
respect—not only allowed on the master's bed, but given a special pillow so they could sleep
between Hitch and his wife. Often they seemed to take on his character as well: irascible but not
without humor—able to scoff at and mug for the press at the same time.*

R O B I N   S C H W A R T Z
C H I N E S E   C R E S T E D ,   1 9 9 3

This was taken at the Westminster Dog Show. Even though
the breed is Chinese, it reminds me of Mexican Hairless dogs.

O V E R L E A F :   P E R - O L L E   S T A C K M A N
S T O C K H O L M   A R C H I P E L A G O ,   1 9 8 0

Lawan was one of the few expert divers in the dog kingdom.
His name in Swedish has to do with something lovely.
His owner was a professional diver. Everytime his master went
diving, Lawan would try to follow him and nearly drown
in the process. So my friend fashioned some dog-sized
equipment and taught Lawan how to dive. Lawan wore
the tank, the mask—everything. He wore boots here so
he wouldn't scratch our wetsuits accidentally when we were
all underwater. He was crazy about diving.

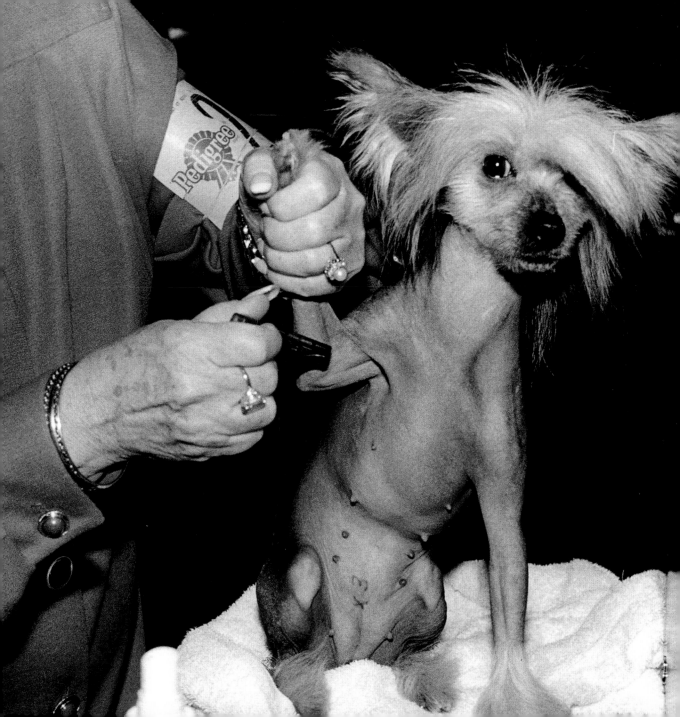

SUSAN COPEN OKEN
MASTIFF, 1989

The dog was backstage, in the benching area at the Westminster Kennel Club.
His handler was really working hard. Much harder than he was.

JOYCE RAVID
POODLE YAWNING, 1980